Skira**M**ini**ART**books

Francesca Marini

TINTORETTO

Skira editore
SkiraMiniARTbooks

Editor
Eileen Romano

Design
Marcello Francone

Editorial Coordination
Giovanna Rocchi

Layout
Anna Cattaneo

Editing
Maria Conconi

Iconographical Research
Marta Tosi

Translation
Robert Burns for Language
Consulting Congressi, Milan

First published in Italy in 2010
by Skira Editore S.p.A.
Palazzo Casati Stampa
via Torino 61
20123 Milano
Italy

www.skira.net

Printed and bound in Italy.
First edition

ISBN 978-88-572-0551-9

Front cover
Mercury and the Graces
(detail), 1577–78
Palazzo Ducale, Sala
dell'Anticollegio, Venice

Facing title page
Last Supper (detail), 1578–81
Scuola Grande di San Rocco,
Sala Grande Superiore, Venice

On page 86
*Saint Mark's Body brought
to Venice* (detail), 1563–64
Gallerie dell'Accademia, Venice

Contents

Tintoretto

On May 31, 1594, "master Jacomo Robusti, known as Tintoretto, 75 years old" died after "fifteen days of fever". His birth may thus be dated to 1519, the year that marked the beginning of the Protestant Reformation, which would lead to the fervour of the Counter-Reformation. The precise artistic dictates of this latter movement would not find expression until after the conclusion of the Council of Trent in 1563, but the Counter-Reformation would leave its mark on religious life prior to that, starting in Tintoretto's childhood, the artist who would be defined in modern times as the religious painter *par excellence*.

Tintoretto's father, Giovanni Battista, not only brought him into the world but also provided the reason for the artist's nickname. Giovanni was a *tintore* (dyer) and given that Jacopo apparently was barely "five feet" tall, he was given the diminutive appellation of "tintoretto" (little dyer). It also appears that Giovanni Battista's fabric dyeing workshop had attained a stature that granted its proprietor commercial privileges and the right to assume public functions as a "citizen" and not as a mere "commoner" of the Republic of Venice. The intellectual climate at Battista's house must thus have been rather lively, with Jacopo being directed toward the painting trade and his brother, Domenico, becoming a musician at the Gonzaga court in Mantua.

By 1539, Tintoretto would have finished his apprenticeship in one or more Venetian botteghe – it is not known in which – and become an independent *depentor* (painter). There is no proof that he was in Titian's workshop or house to "follow his examples", as Carlo Ridolfi claimed, and indeed the early works of the young artist show other influences. According to Ridolfi, Titian, feeling "a pang of jealousy" and "a threat to his honour", sent the young Tintoretto away after seeing his first notable drawings. However, instead of giving us some viable clues to Tintoretto's actual apprenticeship, it seems that, in conjuring this conflict between Titian and Tintoretto, Ridolfi exploited a recurrent motif in art history: the difficult encounter between an affirmed artist and a rising star. Indeed, Titian's disapproval may be cited in explaining the rupture between Pietro Aretino and Tintoretto after 1548, Titian always having been very close to Aretino. Doubtlessly, Tintoretto's rapid rise in the Venetian artistic scene of the time and his autonomy from Titian did not win him the good graces of the older master, who saw his unrivalled pre-eminence in Venice threatened by the young upstart. However, it may also be said that it was Tintoretto's enterprising ambition, which at times bordered on impropriety, that provided the spark for the first controversies, arising especially out of the methods he adopted in wangling an increasing number of commissions.

Saint Mary of Egypt (detail), 1582–87 Scuola Grande di San Rocco, Sala Terrena, Venice

While Tintoretto was creating the first works in his studio on Campo San Cassian around 1540, Venice, one of Europe's most cosmopolitan cities and a centre for intellectuals and politicians, was welcoming some of the major and most advanced representatives of Tuscan-Roman artistic culture, almost all of them passing through the house of Pietro Aretino. There were many stimuli for the young Tintoretto. Having thoroughly studied casts of the most famous ancient and modern sculpture, and the masters Michelangelo and Raphael through drawings, copies and especially prints, which represented a vast source of learning on technique and a trove of models, Tintoretto dated a *Sacra Conversazione* "1540" and signed it "Jachobus", his first known autographic work. The years spent in his bottega in the Campo San Cassian, in the heart

of town, were filled with study and work, also handicrafts. Between the San Cassian and Rialto districts were located the docks for canal crossings and upriver traffic. The zone was a bustle of commercial activity, which would often be depicted at the margins of Tintoretto's religious and mythological subjects.

A likely hypothesis is that the young artist travelled to Mantua in this period, a city that had been redecorated by Giulio Romano, who was considered the heir to Raphael. This would be supported by the correspondence between the perspective views adopted by Tintoretto in the fourteen octagonal panels depicting episodes drawn from Ovid's *Metamorphoses* decorating a ceiling in the palazzo of the Counts Pisani di San Paterniano in Venice with those on the ceiling of the Sala di Psiche in Palazzo Te in Mantua. Giulio Romano had developed and refined a very efficacious system to guide him in his figurations, a system that, according to Ridolfi, Tintoretto also used in his early years as an artist. To paint foreshortened figures, the artist "hung models by ropes from the ceiling beams in order to observe the effect of viewing them from below", so as to be able to directly study the poses and avoid gross errors of perspective. Additionally, to achieve the desired effects of "light and shadow", Tintoretto fashioned "small models in wax or clay", dressed them "in rags, carefully seeking to recreate the limbs through the folds in the cloth" and then put them in "small houses or perspectives composed of boards and paper, placing small candles at the windows". It was perhaps precisely in this manner that he resolved the issue of the distribution of sources of light on two different planes in *The Wise and Foolish Virgins* (Museum Boijmans Van Beuningen,

Last Supper (detail), 1592–94 San Giorgio Maggiore, Venice

Rotterdam), painted around 1546. Ridolfi also tells us that in those years Tintoretto continued the work as a decorator, with other artists who painted and sold, under the arcades ringing Piazza San Marco, pieces of furniture executed in the styles of the most famous masters. This was an artisanal type of painting intended for easy sales, albeit being conceived for aristocratic patrons. An example is the series of ornamental panels depicting Biblical scenes, probably for use in chests, painted by Tintoretto in 1543–44 and now found in the Kunsthistorisches Museum of Vienna. In addition to their references to the pictorial tradition of Bonifacio de' Pitati, the six scenes also exhibit Tintoretto's interest for another artist, Andrea Schiavone, among the first in Venice to accept and develop the novelties of the Tuscan-Roman figurative culture. It is in fact from this Dalmatian painter that Tintoretto would have gained the technique of the more rapid and fluid touch and freer brushstrokes that would characterise his mature pictorial language. This affinity with the brushstroke and also with the elongated and sinuous figures of Schiavone would be repeated in the case for a spinet depicting *Women Playing Music* (1545–46, Museo di Castelvecchio, Verona) and in works conceived by Tintoretto for other purposes, such as the *Conversion of Saint Paul* (1544) in Washington.

In February 1545, Tintoretto received the first of the letters from Pietro Aretino that have survived to the present day. Aretino wanted to thank him for two ceiling paintings, now lost, depicting "the fable of Apollo and Marsyas" and "the novella of Argus and Hermes". We thus know that at that date the artist had already worked for one of the most powerful men on the Italian peninsula and that the work had been much applauded. His path now opened before him. Tintoretto had achieved a freshness and naturalness much appreciated by Pietro

12

in the stories painted on the "ceiling of his bedroom" in his palazzo. While the figures in the canvas of *Christ Washing His Disciples' Feet* (Newcastle-upon-Tyne) are certainly "beautiful", a more significant attribute is their "lifelike and vital" qualities as described by Aretino in reference to his "stories". They are figures that readily refer to the types of people who populated the city in those times. The apostles, evoking the people of the street resting on plank-beds in the inns, and the people around the table are expressively and distinctly characterised, with poses that, while adhering to precise schemas drawn from the repertory of studies of Pordenone, Michelangelo and Giulio Romano, maintain total allegiance with a realistic and popular figuration. Drawing directly on the spontaneity of sentiments and immediacy of actions of the contemporary events portrayed in the theatre of Andrea Calmo, a man of letters, poet and playwright of the time, Tintoretto brought living and pulsating representations to the canvas, going even beyond the playwright's naturalism. It was an anti-rhetorical poetics promoted initially by Aretino, who openly championed the young Tintoretto, at least since 1545, and would seal his affirmation in 1548 with *The Miracle of Saint Mark*, in which Aretino himself was metaphorically honoured with the insertion of a vivid portrait of him in profile among the participants in the scene.

It was Marco Episcopi – father of the "beloved" Faustina, who would become the painter's wife in 1553 – who commissioned Tintoretto to paint *The Miracle of Saint Mark* in 1547 when he was Guardian Grande of the Scuola Grande di San Marco. The confraternity of San Marco, who were dedicated to religious and charitable (not educational) activities like the other Scuole Grandi of the Most Serene Republic of Venice (the *Serenissima*), commissioned the first

13

in a series of paintings dedicated to Saint Mark. It was placed in the space between two windows on the wall overlooking the Campo dei Santi Giovanni e Paolo in the Sala Capitolare of the Albergo, a hall used as an audience chamber and treasury.

Right from the start, *The Miracle of Saint Mark* created quite an impression, attracting many curious onlookers and eliciting much praise but also significant criticism. Just a few years prior to 1548, Sansovino had completed a bronze bas-relief for the left-hand choir of St. Mark's Basilica, with the same subject. He had centred the miraculous event on the sudden arrival of the saint flying down from on high to smash the instruments of the slave's martyrdom. The theme of the miracle was inspired by the *Legenda Aurea* of Jacobus de Varagine, but the detail of the saint descending in flight was completely new. For his *Miracle*, Tintoretto proposed not only the same interpretation, but also the same compositional layout as had been used by Sansovino. This may certainly be interpreted as due homage from a younger artist to the authoritative figure of an older and acclaimed one. Indeed, Sansovino was the author of the main altar in the Scuola di San Marco.

Christ in the House of Martha and Mary (detail), *circa* 1565 Alte Pinakothek, Munich

Tintoretto incorporated a reference to the work of the official architect of the *Serenissima* into a composition intensely vivified by the extreme gestural and expressive qualities of its figures, by the bright colours of their clothing and the variety of hairdos, embroidery, coats of mail and armours all shining in the ray of light falling upon the group gathered around the prostate slave, with the right-hand portion of the pictorial space left in shadow. As Aretino wrote, "the spectacle" appeared "more real than fictional", and anyone even "scarcely versed

14

in the virtues of drawing" could only be amazed at the slave's "living body (…) which, completely nude (…) is offered up to the cruelty of martyrdom". That naked figure, made of "flesh", was the fruit of long years of practice in drawing from live models and studies of anatomy. We know that Tintoretto "skinned the limbs of cadavers to see how the muscles worked underneath, learning how to match that which he observed in relief with the natural thing". He had already undertaken these studies and copies in his studio in Campo San Cassian and continued to produce them also in the new studio near the church of San

Moses striking the Rock (detail), 1575–77 Scuola Grande di San Rocco, Sala Grande Superiore, Venice

Marziale, where he certainly completed *The Miracle of Saint Mark*. Following the success of this work, his studio was soon teeming with helpers on enormous canvases and monumental altarpieces for the preeminent Venetian confraternities and churches. The same year he completed the *Miracle*, Tintoretto had begun work for the church of San Marziale, producing the altarpiece with the patron saint in glory between St. Peter and St. Paul, for which he received payment in December 1549, and a number of works in the choir chapel in 1551, which have never been found.

In the meantime, in late 1549 Tintoretto completed a second painting for the church of San Rocco that would definitively mark the importance of his work among the painting of his time. In exchange for admission to the confraternity, "in addition to the fee paid", Tintoretto delivered a *telero* (large format canvas) nearly seven metres wide depicting *Saint Rocco curing the Plague-Stricken* for the homonymous church. After *The Miracle of Saint Mark*, the painter opened up to new pursuits focussing mainly on light. In the representation of *Saint Rocco curing the Plague-Stricken* an intensely dramatic and surreal luminarism

17

disrupts the nocturnal obscurity of the "hospital filled with beds and sick persons in various attitudes", highlighting "some nude figures very well conceived, and a dead body in foreshortening that is very beautiful" – as Vasari wrote after his second visit to Venice – as well as the creased flesh, grimaces and suffering of the sick, and the powerful chiaroscuro effects of flesh lit up by reds and cooled by greens. One year before Tintoretto completed the work for San Rocco, Titian had begun his *Martyrdom of Saint Lawrence*, which was placed on the altar of the church of the Crociferi in 1549. Tintoretto would thus have easily been able to study the latest achievement of the master. But, more than a strenuous chase after avant-garde innovations, what united Tintoretto with other painters of the period was the luminaristic quest, which would lead to a transformation of the Renaissance relation between light and setting. This began in the Venetian figurative arts with Titian's *Martyrdom of Saint Lawrence* and continued with *Saint Rocco curing the Plague-Stricken*.

Adoration of the Shepherds (detail), 1578–81
Scuola Grande
di San Rocco, Sala Grande
Superiore, Venice

At the beginning of the 1560s, it had become indispensable for Tintoretto to unite "talent" and "facility" or speed. The "praticon de man" (someone who is more successful than talented), as Marco Boschini would later call him, began turning out works at a faster and faster pace, aided by a bottega that grew progressively over the years. Around 1550, he created altarpieces for several Venetian churches and one for San Michele in Vicenza and, in the years 1550–53, the four stories of Genesis for the Scuola della Santissima Trinità, where he developed a new conception in the relationship between the figure and natural

18

landscape: *The Creation of the Animals*, *Adam and Eve*, *Cain and Abel* and *Adam and Eve before the Eternal* exhibit a landscape emanating the same vitalism that animates the figures.

The organ shutters for the church of the Madonna dell'Orto, three canvases for the Sala del Magistrato del Sale in the Palazzo dei Camerlenghi and the decoration of other organ shutters for the church of Santa Maria del Giglio were only some of the major commissions Tintoretto completed by 1555 before wrestling another, given by the fathers of the church of the Crociferi, from Paolo Veronese.

Around 1553, Jacopo married Faustina Episcopi, the daughter of the man to whom he owed the commission for the Scuola di San Marco. Marietta, the first of his eight children, who would become a painter and work with her father, was perhaps already born in 1554. The upkeep of the bottega, his family and the rent of forty-two ducats for the house in San Marziale must have represented a significant burden on the painter's finances. Having decided to obtain, by any means necessary, the commission that had already been granted to Veronese, Tintoretto "was able to talk them into giving him the commission, promising them that he would paint it in the manner of Veronese so that it would be thought to be by his hand". The Fathers of the church of the Crociferi capitulated before such insistence and, as Ridolfi continues, Tintoretto "well proved that he knew how to paint in any fashion, transforming himself as pleased his patrons". In the *Assumption of the Virgin* he showed he understood and knew well how to achieve Veronese's lightened colour schemes and his elegant and decorative Titianesque plasticism. The diffused luminosity and the choice of cold, vivacious and very light colours are a few of the characteristics that Tintoretto borrowed from Veronese. His *Virgin* takes flight supported by angels in a

20

whirl of clouds dotted with cherubims and, in the lower section of the altarpiece, apostles are arranged in a semicircle around the sepulchre in poses that theatrically contribute to emphasise the rapt wonder of their expressions. While vivified and deranged by its spinning rotation, the composition derives from one Titian had ideated for the analogous subject fifty years earlier for the church of the Frari. However, the orange, the dark blue highlighted with azure, the green of the mantles and clothing have a brightness and intensity that, along with the limpid sky streaked with white clouds, appear deliberately introduced by Tintoretto in order to please the Fathers by emulating Veronese's style.

But for the "most tremendous brain ever had by a painter", the step from imitation to assimilation was a short one, as he would prove with a work that "had everyone running" to see it at Casa Correr and is now at the National Gallery in London. Marco Boschini describes Tintoretto's *Saint George and the Dragon* thus:

"It is Saint George on horseback strong and right / who sets out boldly lance at rest / slays the dragon and the queen distressed / is snatched from death and freed of fright".

Boschini writes that "everything moves and jumps" in Tintoretto's work. But precisely because the artist maintains a rational organisation in his multiplication of space, it produces a "sense of dizziness" induced by the increasing dynamism of scenes immersed in gorges of shadow and light. This dynamic and convulsed conception of space characterises *Christ curing the Paralytic*, painted by Tintoretto in 1559 for the church of San Rocco. The work, depicting a miracle of Christ, decorated the doors of the silverware cabinet. The artist had now reached full maturity and the years from 1562 to 1566 witnessed such a production of works that he certainly needed helpers and appren-

21

tices in his workshop, amongst which predominated, oddly enough, Flemings and Germans.

In the short span of four years, Tintoretto completed the two large canvases of the church of the Madonna dell'Orto and the Stories for the Scuola di San Marco, and began work on the San Rocco series and the first paintings for San Cassian. In addition he also kept working as a portraitist, a trade he had conducted since his early years as a *depentor* on Campo San Cassian. Tintoretto had always painted portraits from live models, depicting his patrons in his canvases and creating official portraits. He thus became the portraitist of Venetian society of his time. Alongside dogi, senators and a rich array of admirals, nobles, ladies, literati and ecclesiastics, he also painted some of the best known courtesans of the time. He created an entire gallery of figures representing the political and intellectual spheres of sixteenth-century Venice, among which courtesans, such as Veronica Franco, were prominent figures. An assiduous *habituée* of Casa Venier, the home of one of Venice's most illustrious families and meeting ground for literati, poets and the most famous composers and musicians, Veronica had had an affair with Henry III of France and dedicated her *Terze rime* to Guglielmo Gonzaga, duke of Mantua. Her portrait painted by Tintoretto has been lost, but we still have the words of the courtesan-poet in a letter to the artist: "When I saw my portrait, the work of your divine hand, I was left wondering a while if it was a painting or a ghost conjured before me by some diabolical trickery". Tintoretto also portrayed courtesans as pagan goddesses, with mythological attributes and elements clearly referring to their elegant lifestyles. Flora, Leda and Danae are

Frederick II conquers Parma (detail), 1579–80
Alte Pinakothek, Munich

23

some of the subjects in whose guises appear courtesans easily recognisable by the strings of pearls around their necks, by the combs, jewellery or mirrors frequently associated with such persons.

In the years 1562–63, for a mere one hundred ducats, Tintoretto created the decorative complex for the choir of the church of the Madonna dell'Orto, which included two enormous *teleri* more than fourteen metres high portraying the *Worship of the Golden Calf* and the *Last Judgement*, and the decorations for five sections of the choir with the *Virtues*. As in other cases, he played on the contrast between the two scenes, conceiving the *Worship* as a static scene marked by the orderly superimposition of figuratively distinct zones, and the *Judgement* as a complex and whirling composition where the artful use of light coordinates a copious array of figures. Although Titian's *Gloria* (Prado, Madrid) provided Tintoretto with a precedent for his arrangement of figures along diagonals, Michelangelo's *Last Judgement* must unquestionably be considered an ultimate source, a point of departure for certain technical and thematic derivations. But Tintoretto breaks away from this, replacing the rotational rhythm of Michelangelo's space with the ascension and fall of groups of figures, deepening the space of the composition.

While Tintoretto was completing work on the choir in the Madonna dell'Orto, in 1562 Tommaso Rangone, a doctor and scholar who was at the time Guardian Grande of the Scuola di San Marco, asked the assembly of his fellow brothers for permission to commission, "at his own expense", three paintings of the miracles of the patron saint of the School and the representation of the seven deadly sins juxtaposed against the seven theological virtues.

More than a decade after his *Miracle of Saint Mark*, Tintoretto came back to work for the Scuola di San Marco, establishing himself as the painter who best knew how to communicate the message of Christian faith. In 1566, Giorgio Vasari saw the completed *teleri*: Tintoretto had depicted the *Finding of the Body of Saint Mark in Alexandria* (Brera, Milan), *Saint Mark's Body brought to Venice* and *Saint Mark saving a Saracen from Shipwreck*, both at the Gallerie dell'Accademia in Venice.

At the height of his activity, he was also able to gain another important commission by outmanoeuvring his competitors, and not in the most irreprehensible of ways. In 1557, the Council of the Scuola Grande di San Rocco decided to allocate two hundred ducats per year to the decoration of the Sala dell'Albergo. Some time later, in 1564, during another council meeting, the decision was taken to decorate the ceiling of the hall at the expense of the brothers. On May 31 of that year, the Guardian Grande of the Scuola called a contest among a number of painters living in Venice, inviting them to submit a project for the central oval on the ceiling. But just three weeks later, Jacopo Tintoretto presented his oval with the *Glory of Saint Rocco*, offering it as a gift to the confraternity, in spite of the efforts of Zani di Zignoni, who had declared himself willing to personally contribute fifteen ducats provided that Tintoretto did not take part in the decoration.

The oval was immediately placed on the ceiling and Tintoretto declared also that he was ready to provide the other paintings for the Sala dell'Albergo, free of charge, asking only that his expenses be covered. In June the Council met again to decide if this gift could be accepted. It was only after Tintoretto was accepted into the Scuola as a brother that he was given the commission to decorate the entire ceiling and the walls, with eighty-one votes in favour and nineteen against.

In the space of a year, Tintoretto completed the *Crucifixion* on the back wall of the hall. This would be followed, before the close of 1567, by three *teleri* with the *Stories of the Passion* on the entry wall, as well as the two *Prophets* between the windows on the side walls. Over the span of twenty-three years, the artist completed some fifty canvases for the Scuola di San Rocco, starting in the Sala dell'Albergo with the *Passion of Christ* and continuing on, harmoniously uniting motifs from the Old and New Testaments, to celebrate the charitable aims of the School in honour of the saint who protected against the worst affliction of the times, the plague.

In these years, Tintoretto was assisted in his work by his second-born son, Domenico, who achieved notable fame in his father's footsteps, as did another of Jacopo's sons, Marco.

Rape of Helen
(detail), 1580–85
Museo Nacional
del Prado, Madrid

The same religious pathos that informed the canvases of San Rocco seems also to underlie the conception of the large *telero* of the *Last Judgement* that Tintoretto created for the Sala dello Scrutinio in Palazzo Ducale, which was destroyed in the fire of 1577. According to Ridolfi, "the motif of that painting had such impact as to awe the souls beholding it". After doing the decorations for the ceiling of the Atrium and the Saletta degli Inquisitori, Tintoretto received this prestigious commission around 1570 directly from the Republic of Venice. He was already an established figure in Catholicism, not only in the churches but especially among the confraternities. His work as a portraitist would bring him increasingly in contact with those in power, and he aspired to becoming the official painter of the *Serenissima*, given that Titian was nearing the venerable old age of eighty.

26

In spite of his age, the artist from the Cadore region remained the first painter of the State and the Senate turned to him for the commemoration of the Battle of Lepanto, during which, allied with the Pope and Philip II of Spain, Venice had defeated the Turkish fleet in 1571. But once again, Tintoretto was able to prevail, offering to do the work for free. He expressed his intention to the Doge Alvise Mocenigo, whose portrait he had painted together with his family, to accept the work "with no profit at all, deeming (…) sufficient the reward of having known how to serve his Prince well". Within a year, as promised, he completed the work, which unfortunately was another of those destroyed in the fire of December 1577.

Massacre of the Innocents (detail), 1582–87 Scuola Grande di San Rocco, Sala Terrena, Venice

In many of the paintings Tintoretto planned the composition, traced out the preparatory sketches for the individual figures and then oversaw the execution by his helpers. Starting in the 1570s, prominent amongst these assistants were Tintoretto's own children. His favourite, Marietta, was raised on art and music from her birth. One of her works is a self-portrait with harpsichord and sheet music. Domenico was born in 1560 and Marco one year later.

In 1576, in the midst of the plague that would claim the elderly Titian among its victims, the Council of the Scuola di San Rocco accepted Tintoretto's proposal to create a painting for the ceiling of the Sala Grande Superiore and chose the theme of Moses and the bronze serpent. The Biblical episode was perfectly apt. In it, by God's mercy, Moses sets a bronze serpent upon a staff and shows it to his people as a source of salvation, bringing about the miracle of the healing of the sick. The *Bronze Serpent* was delivered for the festival of San Rocco, the 16th of August, and was the first canvas in the series exe-

29

cuted to decorate the entire room, starting with the ceiling and themes from the Old Testament and continuing with the walls and episodes from the New. In a letter dated 27 November 1577 to the School, Tintoretto "seeking to express his great love" for the "venerable school" and his devotion to "the glorious" San Rocco, undertook to deliver three paintings a year for the festival of the saint in exchange for an annuity of one hundred ducats.

The *Fasti Gonzagheschi* created for Duke Guglielmo Gonzaga are eight *teleri* portraying political and military events featuring the Gonzagas in the fifteenth and sixteenth centuries. As documented in a letter from Paolo Moro, the duke's ambassador to Venice, the first four were initiated in late 1578, completed in March of the following year and placed in the Sala dei Marchesi of the Palazzo Ducale in Mantua. Then, on 1 October 1579, Teodoro Sangiorgio, the superintendent of works in the Palazzo, wrote to Paolo Moro with a commission for four additional *teleri*, which were completed on 10 May 1580. In September, the painter and his wife, Faustina, were in Mantua, where his brother Domenico lived, to witness the placement of the works in the Sala dei Duchi of the Palazzo.

Annunciation
(detail), 1582–87
Scuola Grande
di San Rocco,
Sala Terrena, Venice

With *Victory at Lepanto* painted for the Sala dello Scrutinio in the Palazzo Ducale of Venice and later destroyed in the fire of 1577, Tintoretto initiated a genre that would also find expression in the *Fasti Gonzagheschi* and the *Rape of Helen* in the Prado. This series of exemplars would constitute the thematic base for the development of battle paintings, which would be a dominant theme in the recreation of the decorative cycles in Palazzo Ducale after the fires of 1574 and

1577. As in other works at the Palazzo, Tintoretto's bottega did a massive amount of work for the ceiling and, according to Ridolfi, some contemporaries did not like the canvases, judging them "conducted with little study". Some painters, continues Ridolfi, took up Tintoretto's defence, hiding "among the seats to hear what was being said about him and occasionally speaking up for him so that once the persecution was over, the painting, to the glory of its author, was favourably established in the minds of all".

For the Sala del Senato, restored after the damage suffered in 1574, Tintoretto was charged with painting the grandiose ceiling with the *Venice, Queen of the Sea*, dated between 1587 and 1594. It was an ambitious work, one that marked the final creative moment of the master, one where he attempted to confer almost a cosmic value upon the open space in which are suspended the divinities bearing witness to triumphant Venice.

The Senate had decided after the fire that Guariento's *Paradise* in the *Sala del Maggior Consiglio* had to be redone but we do not know how the choice of final model was reached, i.e., whether a competition was called or if arrangements were made privately. According to Ridolfi, the choice fell to Paolo Veronese and Francesco Bassano, "but since their different manners of painting were hard to reconcile and also since Paolo died soon thereafter, neither of them began on the work (…). In the end it was assigned to Tintoretto".

As Ridolfi has recorded, Tintoretto's immense canvas was painted, divided into two parts, in the old Scuola della Misericordia and the painter, "not able to withstand, burdened by his years, such long fatigue", availed himself greatly of the help of his son Domenico. With his *Paradise* Tintoretto concluded his work as a "State" painter, a participant in the great efforts made by *La Serenissima* when the signs of decadence were beginning to appear on the horizon after the ephemeral victory at Lepanto.

F or the presbytery of the church of San Giorgio Maggiore, which was being built in 1589, Tintoretto painted *The Jews in the Desert* and the *Last Supper*, both completed in 1594, the year of his death. In the first *telero* the composition is divided into many different episodes, while in the left background the compact crowd presents itself in the form of a choir, executed in a fluid and loose medium. The scene is painted in the open air but in a cold light, different from the "tenebrosity" characterising the artist's late work. While food for the body constitutes the overt narrative, it is that of the soul that represents the allegorical theme of the *Last Supper*, which may be considered Tintoretto's last great masterpiece.

Perhaps one of the last works by the painter was the *Deposition of Christ* in the Cappella dei Morti in San Giorgio Maggiore. The chapel was begun in 1592 and documents show that Tintoretto was paid for it seventy ducats in 1594. We may thus date the execution of the painting to this period. It is quite a suggestive work both for its luminaristic qualities and for its abbreviated and fragmentary pictorial form, which concludes the activity of the prolific Venetian painter as a sort of spiritual testament.

On 30 May 1594, anticipating the end, Tintoretto dictated his testament. He died the following day. His death marked the passing of the last of the great protagonists of sixteenth-century Venetian painting.

Works

1. *Christ and the Adulteress*, circa 1546

2. *Athena and Arachne*,
1543–44

3. *Venus and Adonis*,
1543–44

37

4. *The Miracle of Saint Mark* (detail and entire work), 1547–48

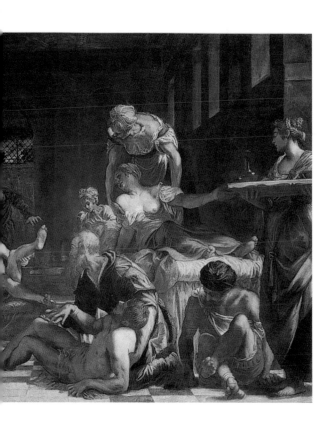

5. *San Rocco curing the Plague-Stricken*, 1549

Following pages
6. *The Creation of the Animals*, 1550–53

7. *Portrait of Procurator Jacopo Soranzo*, circa 1550

8. *Portrait of Caterina Sandella*, circa 1550–55

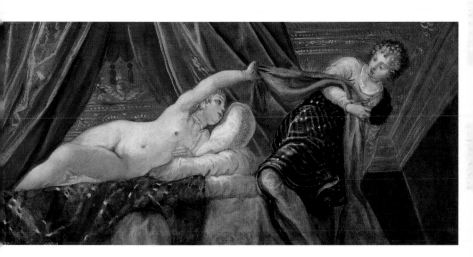

9. *Cain and Abel*, 1550–53

10. *Joseph and the Wife of Putifarre, circa* 1555

47

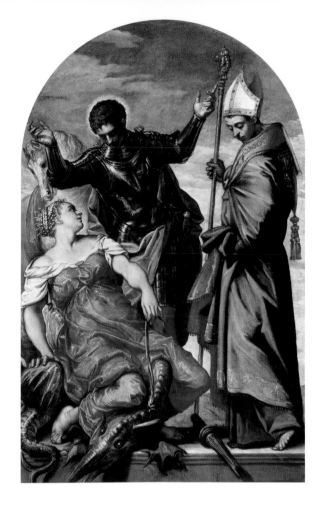

11. *The Evangelists Mark and John,* circa 1552–57 (1553?)

12. *The Princess, Saint George and Saint Louis of Toulouse,* 1553

13. *Presentation of the*
Virgin in the Temple,
circa 1552–53

14. *The Miracle of the
Loaves and Fishes*
(entire work and detail),
circa 1555

15. *Deposition of Christ,
circa* 1559–60

16. *Christ in the House
of Martha and Mary, circa*
1565

17. *Portrait of a Gentleman with Gold Chain, circa* 1560

18. *Portrait of Alvise Cornaro, circa* 1560–62

56

19. *Finding of the Body of Saint Mark in Alexandria*, 1563–64

20. *Saint Mark's Body brought to Venice*, 1563–64

21. *The Trinity,*
circa 1564–68

22. *Pietà*, 1563–71

IACHOPO TAT... ...TI SANSOVIN...

23. *Portrait of Jacopo Sansovino, circa* 1566

24. *Portrait of a Warrior, circa* 1570–75

25. *Moses striking
the Rock*, circa 1577

26. *Elisha multiplies
the Bread*, 1577–78

27. *Minerva repelling Mars from Peace and Prosperity*, 1577–78

28. *Mercury and the Graces*, 1577–78

29. *Bacchus and Ariadne*,
1577–78

30. *Leda and the Swan*,
circa 1578

69

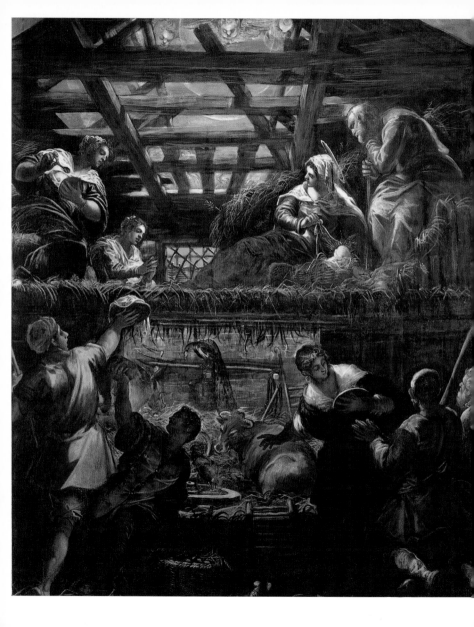

31. *Adoration of the Shepherds*, 1578–81

32. *Christ curing the Paralytic*, 1578–81

33. *The Miracle of the*
Loaves and Fishes, 1578–81

34. *Last Supper*, 1578–81

73

35. *Agony in the Garden*,
1578–81

36. *Resurrection*, 1578–81

37. *Frederick II conquers Parma*, 1579–80

38. *Rape of Helen*, 1580–85

39. *Annunciation*, 1582–87

40. *Adoration of the Magi*,
1582–87

79

41. *Flight into Egypt*,
1582–87

42. *Massacre of the
Innocents*, 1582–87

43. *The Jews in the Desert*, 1592–94

44. *Last Supper*, 1592–94

83

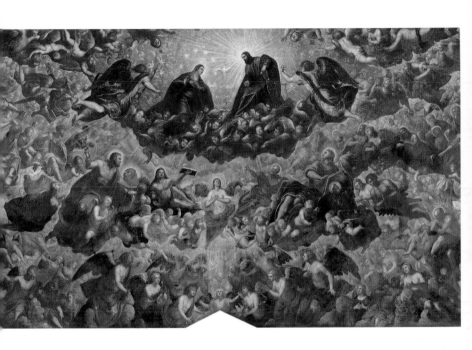

45. *Venice, Queen
of the Sea*, 1587–94

46. *Paradise*, 1588–92

Appendix

Catalogue of the Works

1. *Christ and the Adulteress,* *circa* 1546
Oil on canvas, 118.5 x 168 cm
Galleria Nazionale d'Arte Antica, Palazzo Barberini, Rome

2. *Athena and Arachne,* 1543–44
Oil on canvas, 145 x 272 cm
Galleria degli Uffizi, Contini Bonacossi Collection, Florence

3. *Venus and Adonis,* 1543–44
Oil on canvas, 145 x 272 cm
Galleria degli Uffizi, Contini Bonacossi Collection, Florence

4. *The Miracle of Saint Mark,* 1547–48
Oil on canvas, 416 x 544 cm
Gallerie dell'Accademia, Venice

5. *San Rocco curing the Plague-Stricken,* 1549
Oil on canvas, 307 x 673 cm
Church of San Rocco, Venice

6. *The Creation of the Animals,* 1550–53
Oil on canvas, 151 x 258 cm
Gallerie dell'Accademia, Venice

7. *Portrait of Procurator Jacopo Soranzo, circa* 1550
Oil on canvas, 106 x 90 cm
Gallerie dell'Accademia, Venice

8. *Portrait of Caterina Sandella, circa* 1550–55
Oil on canvas, 114 x 100 cm
Private collection, Venice

9. *Cain and Abel,* 1550–53
Oil on canvas, 149 x 196 cm
Gallerie dell'Accademia, Venice

10. *Joseph and the Wife of Putifarre, circa* 1555
Oil on canvas, 54 x 117 cm
Museo Nacional del Prado, Madrid

11. *The Evangelists Mark and John, circa* 1552–57 (1553?)
Oil on canvas, 257 x 150 cm
Church of Santa Maria del Giglio, Venice

12. *The Princess, Saint George and Saint Louis of Toulouse,* 1553
Oil on canvas, 226 x 146 cm
Gallerie dell'Accademia, Venice

13. *Presentation of the Virgin in the Temple, circa* 1552–53
Oil on canvas, 429 x 480 cm
Church of the Madonna dell'Orto, Venice

14. *The Miracle of the Loaves and Fishes, circa* 1555
Oil on canvas, 118 x 140 cm
Private collection

15. *Deposition of Christ, circa* 1559–60
Oil on canvas, 227 x 294 cm
Gallerie dell'Accademia, Venice

16. *Christ in the House of Martha and Mary, circa* 1565
Oil on canvas, 200 x 132 cm
Alte Pinakothek, Munich

17. *Portrait of a Gentleman with Gold Chain, circa* 1560
Oil on canvas, 103 x 76 cm
Museo Nacional del Prado, Madrid

18. *Portrait of Alvise Cornaro, circa* 1560–62
Oil on canvas, 113 x 85 cm
Galleria Palatina di Palazzo Pitti, Florence

19. *Finding of the Body of Saint Mark in Alexandria,* 1563–64
Oil on canvas, 405 x 405 cm
Pinacoteca di Brera, Milan

20. *Saint Mark's Body brought to Venice,* 1563–64
Oil on canvas, 398 x 315 cm
Venice, Gallerie dell'Accademia

21. *The Trinity, circa* 1564–68
Oil on canvas, 122 x 181 cm
Galleria Sabauda, Turin

22. *Pietà,* 1563–71
Oil on canvas, 108 x 170 cm
Pinacoteca di Brera, Milan

23. *Portrait of Jacopo Sansovino, circa* 1566
Oil on canvas, 70 x 65 cm
Galleria degli Uffizi, Florence

24. *Portrait of a Warrior,* *circa* 1570–75
Oil on canvas, 82 x 67 cm
Madrid, Museo Nacional del Prado

25. *Moses striking the Rock,* *circa* 1577
Oil on canvas, 550 x 520 cm
Scuola Grande di San Rocco, Sala Grande Superiore, Venice

26. *Elisha multiplies the Bread,* 1577–78
Oil on canvas, 370 x 265 cm
Scuola Grande di San Rocco, Sala Grande Superiore, Venice

27. *Minerva repelling Mars from Peace and Prosperity,* 1577–78
Oil on canvas, 148 x 168 cm
Palazzo Ducale, Sala dell'Anticollegio, Venice

28. *Mercury and the Graces,* 1577–78
Oil on canvas, 146 x 155 cm
Palazzo Ducale, Sala dell'Anticollegio, Venice

29. *Bacchus and Ariadne,* 1577–78
Oil on canvas, 146 x 167 cm
Palazzo Ducale, Sala dell'Anticollegio, Venice

30. *Leda and the Swan,* *circa* 1578
Oil on canvas, 162 x 218 cm
Galleria degli Uffizi, Florence

31. *Adoration of the Shepherds,* 1578–81
Oil on canvas, 542 x 455 cm
Scuola Grande di San Rocco, Sala Grande Superiore, Venice

32. *Christ curing the Paralytic,* 1578–81
Oil on canvas, 533 x 529 cm
Scuola Grande di San Rocco, Sala Grande Superiore, Venice

33. *The Miracle of the Loaves and Fishes,* 1578–81
Oil on canvas, 523 x 475 cm
Scuola Grande di San Rocco, Sala Grande Superiore, Venice

34. *Last Supper,* 1578–81
Oil on canvas, 538 x 487 cm
Scuola Grande di San Rocco, Sala Grande Superiore, Venice

35. *Agony in the Garden,* 1578–81
Oil on canvas, 538 x 455 cm
Scuola Grande di San Rocco, Sala Grande Superiore, Venice

36. *Resurrection,* 1578–81
Oil on canvas, 529 x 485 cm
Scuola Grande di San Rocco, Sala Grande Superiore, Venice

37. *Frederick II conquers Parma,* 1579–80
Oil on canvas, 212 x 283.5 cm
Alte Pinakothek, Munich

38. *Rape of Helen,* 1580–85
Oil on canvas, 186 x 307 cm
Museo Nacional del Prado, Madrid

39. *Annunciation,* 1582–87
Oil on canvas, 422 x 545 cm
Scuola Grande di San Rocco, Sala Terrena, Venice

40. *Adoration of the Magi,* 1582–87
Oil on canvas, 425 x 544 cm
Scuola Grande di San Rocco, Sala Terrena, Venice

41. *Flight into Egypt,* 1582–87
Oil on canvas, 422 x 580 cm
Scuola Grande di San Rocco, Sala Terrena, Venice

42. *Massacre of the Innocents,* 1582–87
Oil on canvas, 422 x 546 cm
Scuola Grande di San Rocco, Sala Terrena, Venice

43. *The Jews in the Desert,* 1592–94
Oil on canvas, 377 x 576 cm
Church of San Giorgio Maggiore, Venice

44. *Last Supper,* 1592–94
Oil on canvas, 365 x 568 cm
Church of San Giorgio Maggiore, Venice

45. *Venice, Queen of the Sea,* 1587–94
Oil on canvas, 810 x 420 cm
Palazzo Ducale, Sala del Senato, Venice

46. *Paradise,* 1588–92
Oil on canvas, 700 x 2000 cm
Palazzo Ducale, Sala del Maggior Consiglio, Venice

Life of Tintoretto	Historical events

1519	Year of birth based on information on his death certificate of 31 May 1594 (Venice, State Archives).	Charles V is emperor. The bishop Jacopo Pesaro commissions Titian to paint the altarpiece for the church of Santa Maria Gloriosa dei Frari.
1539	He signs a document dated 22 May "maestro" and has his own studio in Venice on Campo San Cassian.	Pietro Lando is Doge of Venice. Francesco Salviati and his pupil Giuseppe Porta are in Venice. Death of Pordenone.
1540	He paints and signs a *Sacra Conversazione*.	Beginning of the Council of Trent.
1545	He paints two ceilings with mythological subjects for the home of Pietro Aretino.	
1547	He works on *Christ Washing the Disciples' Feet*.	Charles V defeats the Protestant forces in Mühlberg.
1548	Aretino writes to him in April praising the *Miracle of Saint Mark* painted for the Scuola di San Marco in Venice. He accepts a commission to paint the doors of the organ in the church of the Madonna dell'Orto in Venice.	Alessandro Soderini and Lorenzino de' Medici are killed in Venice by assassins hired by Cosimo I, grand duke of Florence. Titian is working on his *Martyrdom of Saint Lawrence* in the church of the Jesuits in Venice.
1549	He paints *Saint Rocco Curing the Plague-Stricken* in the church of San Rocco in Venice.	Pope Paul III dies. Famine causes Venice to be overrun by beggars.
1552	He accepts the commission from procurator Giulio Contarini to paint the doors of the organ in the Venetian church of Santa Maria del Giglio or Zobenigo.	Paolo Veronese is commissioned by Cardinal Ercole Gonzaga to paint *Saint Anthony tempted by the Devil*.
1553	Tintoretto is paid for paintings done for the Ducal Palace in Venice. He marries Faustina Episcopi.	Death of Bonifacio de' Pitati. Veronese begins his work for the Palazzo Ducale in Venice.
1555	He paints the altarpiece with the *Assumption of the Virgin* and *Joseph and the Wife of Putifarre* during or sometime around this year.	Veronese begins decoration of the sacristy of the church of San Sebastiano in Venice.
1556	He is paid the balance for the organ shutters for the church of the Madonna dell'Orto. He paints *Susanna and the Elders* sometime around this year.	Charles V abdicates the throne and is succeeded by Philip II. Decoration work begins on the ceiling of the Libreria Marciana. Death of Pietro Aretino.

90

	Life of Tintoretto	Historical events
1559	He receives payment for *Christ curing the Paralytic*.	The Peace of Cateau-Cambrésis.
1564	He begins work on the Sala dell'Albergo of the Scuola Grande di San Rocco in Venice.	The Venetian senate accepts the decisions of the Council of Trent. Michelangelo dies in Rome.
1568	He paints *Descent of Christ into Limbo* and the *Crucifixion* in his studio on Campo San Cassian in Venice.	The second edition of Giorgio Vasari's *Lives the Artists* is published in Florence.
1571	He receives payment for the *Philosophers* and other paintings executed for the Libreria Marciana.	Battle of Lepanto: Venice and the Holy League defeat the Turks.
1574	He moves into a house on the Fondamenta dei Mori in the parish of San Marziale where he will live for the rest of his life.	Devastating fire in the Palazzo Ducale in Venice.
1575	He begins work on the Sala Grande Superiore of the Scuola di San Rocco.	The plague strikes Venice.
1577	The Scuola di San Rocco accepts Tintoretto's proposal and conditions for continuing to paint for the confraternity.	Another fire in the Venetian Palazzo Ducale. Three paintings by Tintoretto and Titian's *Battle of Cadore* are lost.
1580	He delivers the final four *teleri* of the *Fasti Gonzagheschi* commissioned by Guglielmo Gonzaga for the Palazzo Ducale in Mantua.	Death of Andrea Palladio.
1581	Completion of the canvases for the Sala Grande Superiore of the Scuola di San Rocco.	Torquato Tasso's *Jerusalem Delivered* is published.
1588	He paints his last works for the Scuola di San Rocco.	The first stone is laid for the new Rialto Bridge in Venice. Death of Paolo Veronese.
1592	In or around this year, he paints *The Last Supper* and the *Jews in the Desert* for the presbytery of the church of San Giorgio Maggiore in Venice.	
1594	Tintoretto's death certificate is drawn up on 31 May 1594.	

Critical Anthology

P. Aretino
Letters, IV
To Iacopo, tintore [dyer]. The public acclaim agrees with my own judgement of your large painting dedicated to the Scuola di San Marco, but I go even further in my praise of your extraordinary art. And as there is no nose too cold to smell somehow the scent of incense, there is no man so uneducated in the virtues of design that he would not be amazed at the figure subjected, fully nude and lying on the ground, to the cruelty of martyrdom. His colours are flesh, his lineaments full and his body so alive that I swear, for the love I have for you, that the appearance, air and gazes of the crowd gathered around are so similar to their meaning in that work that the scene appears more real than fashioned. But while this is true, do not let it go to your head, for that would mean you will not seek a higher perfection. And praise to you if you calm the speed of accomplishment into a patience of execution. For slowly but surely the years will bring this about because they, and nothing else, are able to slow the course of negligence, that much overwhelms eager and hasty youth.
Venice, April 1548

G. Vasari
Lives of the Artists, 1568
In the same city of Venice, and about the same time there lived, as he still does, a painter called Jacopo Tintoretto, who has delighted in all the arts, and particularly in playing various musical instruments, besides being agreeable in his every action, but in the matter of painting swift, resolute, fantastic, and extravagant, and the most extraordinary brain that the art of painting has ever produced, as may be seen from all his works and from the fantastic compositions of his scenes, executed by him in a fashion of his own and contrary to the use of other painters. Indeed, he has surpassed even the limits of extravagance with the new and fanciful inventions and the strange vagaries of his intellect, working at haphazard and without design, as if to prove that art is but a jest. This master at times has left as finished works sketches still so rough that the brush-strokes may be seen, done more by chance and vehemence than with judgment and design. He has painted almost every kind of picture in fresco and in oils, with portraits from life, and at every price, insomuch that with these methods he has executed, as he still does, the greater part of the pictures painted in Venice. And since in his youth he proved himself by many beautiful works a man of great judgment, if only he had recognized how great an advantage he had from nature, and had improved it by reasonable study, as has been done by those who have followed the beautiful manners of his predecessors, and had not dashed his work off by mere skill of hand, he would have been one of the greatest painters that Venice has ever had. Not that this prevents him from being a bold and able painter, and delicate, fanciful, and alert in spirit.

R. Longhi
Viatico per cinque secoli di pittura veneziana, 1946
Meanwhile in Venice, precisely when Titian had resolved the greatest conflict within Italian figurative culture in his inner and inimitable drama, Tintoretto was already

raging, characterised enduringly as a *praticon de man* [someone who is more successful than talented] by Boschini, who did not intend thereby to diminish him. And so here it might be worth explaining for what reason Tintoretto's name was violently blazoned some eighty years ago by the romantic Ruskin, together with that of Carpaccio, Bellini and Turner. Perhaps it is because of the fact that in Romanticism, intention and effect are placed on a par. Nor, since then, has there been any easing up—nay, I would say that in the past fifty years, few painters have witnessed more adulation than Tintoretto, even though the reasons were not the same as those motivating Ruskin, at least not until more recent years when they reared their heads again in the most hasty irrationalism. Much earlier than this, it is quite likely that Tintoretto was admired more for his technical skill than for his imagination, especially in Italy, people always being ready to mistake fury for erudition. It was a technical titanism that had appeal in the past two decades. Ojetti urged young artists to learn from Tintoretto how to attack large decorative works. There was indeed a need for a great 'captain of industry' in painting. Such was sought, for painting, in a Piacentini; Tintoretto presented a model that was perhaps too lofty. […] But for this I do not wish to deny Tintoretto his brilliant nature, filled initially with beautiful ideas for dramatic fables to be played out against the scenery of rapidly shifting light and shadow. For this purpose, he used a theatre with mannequins to resolve his luminaristic canvases. Nothing wrong in that. The problem lay in the structure of the mannequins and the mechanism of action that issued forth. When I gaze upon and breathlessly admire, conjuring up a sort of prefigural idea, so to speak, of *Christ*

before Pilate, *Moses striking the Rock* or *Saint Mary of Egypt*, I cannot help immediately imagining what these subjects might have aroused in the hands of an El Greco or a Rembrandt. Why is it, in short, that Tintoretto stands at the canvas and appears at times to be a Vasari or a Zuccari of genius and other times a soulless El Greco? That he had engaged a conflict similar to that with which Titian was grappling around 1540-45 is not in doubt. The sad thing is that he set at it programmatically and resolved it by dint of technical skill. His excogitation of an executive mechanism that achieved an apparent dialectical synthesis between the two extremes of manner and colour amounted simply to the destruction of the passional substance of the two.

A. Chastel
L'art italien, 1956
His effort lies in brandishing expressive instruments of unprecedented vehemence drawing on three forms of Mannerism which appear for the first time to reveal their prodigious resources: the long and sinuous figure which, instead of dissolving into a gilded atmosphere often re-achieves its plastic thrust; the oblique composition rich in vistas; and the light that discolours and works metamorphoses, like a spotlight in the hands of a film director, in a nervous, vibrant and infinitely pathetic universe.

A. Hauser
Der Manierismus, 1964
Under it all, Tintoretto's art is composed of the same elements as that of the painters in the Bologna circle. But while in the latter, with the exception of Tibaldi, the Parmigianino (Francesco Mazzola) vein predominates, in Tintoretto the influence of Michelangelo is stronger and becomes determining for the definitive form of his

style. However, the Parmigianino's formal language remains of fundamental importance for Tintoretto as well and fulfils the dialectical balancing function that fell repeatedly to formalism in the history of Manneristic art. With his own artistic intent, within the dialectic of historical evolution, Tintoretto mainly takes upon himself the task of affirming the expressionistic spiritual forces against the extroverted academicism that dominated the early phase of mature Mannerism, and as a representative of introspective spiritualist art, he gave the second phase the marks that distinguish it. However, he would have contributed to this dialectic in a truly active and fecund way had he not accommodated trends that ran counter to his spiritual values and had these not played an essential part in the development of his style. Tintoretto's position in the history of style is quite complex. While he is a mannerist of Michelangelesque origins, the mannerist qualities in the master's art are not what make the deepest impression on him.

The mannerism of the Parmigianino and also of Vasari and Salviati, who sojourned in Venice around 1540, acted on him in a much more univocal and unilateral fashion, albeit one that was less resolutive in artistic terms, than did that of Michelangelo. In any case, the true heir of the great Roman master is Tintoretto and not international "Michelangelism", from which he kept his distance, in spite of several points of contact.
The true difference between Michelangelo's mannerism and that of Tintoretto lies in the fact that the former embraced relatively limited, while extremely important, mannerist periods, while the latter was and remains a mannerist by nature, notwithstanding certain fluctuations and the intermittence of his stylistic awareness.
While the artist maintained many of the achievements of the mature Renaissance and anticipated certain aspects of the Baroque, he showed none of the "reserve" toward Mannerism as is sometimes attributed to him.

Selected Bibliography

H. Tietze (edited by), *Tintoretto, paintings and drawings*, London 1948

E. Newton (edited by), *Jacopo Tintoretto. The Four Allegories of Venice*, London 1951

A. Hauser, *Der Manierismus: Die Krise der Renaissance und der Ursprung der modernen Kunst*, Monaco 1964

A. Pallucchini, *Tintoretto. The life and work of the artist*, London 1971

A.L. Lepschy, *Tintoretto observed: a documentary survey of critical reactions from the 16th to the 20th century*, Ravenna 1983

C. Ridolfi, *The life of Tintoretto and of his children Domenico and Marietta*, University Park, Pennsylvania 1984

F. Valcanover, *Tintoretto*, New York 1985

T. Nichols, *Tintoretto: the painter and his public*, Norwich 1992

S. Marinelli, *Il ritrovamento del corpo di san Marco di Jacopo Tintoretto*, Milan 1996

D. Rosand, *Painting in sixteenth-century Venice: Titian, Veronese, Tintoretto*, Cambridge 1997

T. Nichols, *Tintoretto: tradition and identity*, London 1999

C. Syre, *Tintoretto: the Gonzaga cycle*, Ostfildern 2000

G. Caputo (edited by), *Tintoretto. Il ciclo di Santa Caterina e la quadreria del palazzo Ducale*, Milan 2005

M. Falomir, *Tintoretto*, London 2007

J. Goldberg, *The seeds of things: theorizing sexuality and materiality in Renaissance representations*, New York 2009

F. Ilchman (edited by), *Titian, Tintoretto, Veronese: rivals in Renaissance Venice*, Aldershot 2009

M.G. Mazzucco, *La lunga attesa dell'angelo*, Milan 2008

M.G. Mazzucco, *Jacomo Tintoretto e i suoi figli. Biografia di una famiglia veneziana*, Milan 2009